iNSPiRED COLOURiNG
FLOWERS

This edition published by Parragon Books Ltd in 2016

Parragon Books Ltd
Chartist House
15–17 Trim Street
Bath BA1 1HA, UK
www.parragon.com

All images courtesy of Shutterstock

Introduction by Dominic Utton
Designed by Karli Skelton
Production by Emily King

ISBN 978-1-4748-1739-4

Printed in China

INSPIRED COLOURING

FLOWERS

COLOURING TO RELAX AND
FREE YOUR MIND

PaRragon

Bath • New York • Cologne • Melbourne • Delhi
Hong Kong • Shenzhen • Singapore

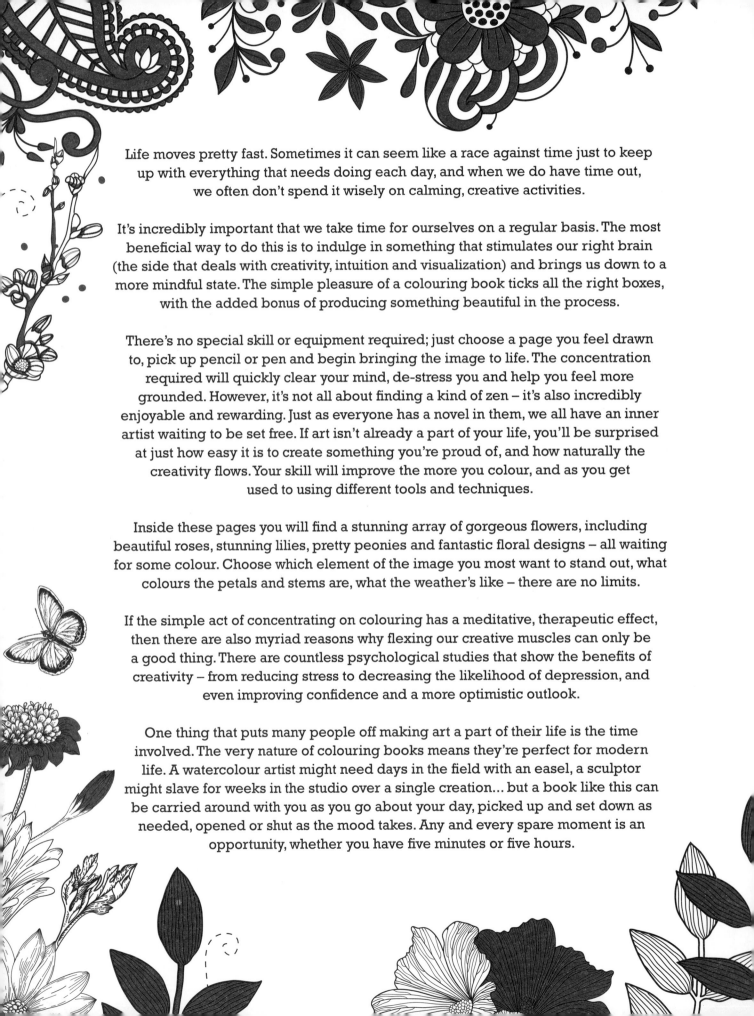

Life moves pretty fast. Sometimes it can seem like a race against time just to keep up with everything that needs doing each day, and when we do have time out, we often don't spend it wisely on calming, creative activities.

It's incredibly important that we take time for ourselves on a regular basis. The most beneficial way to do this is to indulge in something that stimulates our right brain (the side that deals with creativity, intuition and visualization) and brings us down to a more mindful state. The simple pleasure of a colouring book ticks all the right boxes, with the added bonus of producing something beautiful in the process.

There's no special skill or equipment required; just choose a page you feel drawn to, pick up pencil or pen and begin bringing the image to life. The concentration required will quickly clear your mind, de-stress you and help you feel more grounded. However, it's not all about finding a kind of zen – it's also incredibly enjoyable and rewarding. Just as everyone has a novel in them, we all have an inner artist waiting to be set free. If art isn't already a part of your life, you'll be surprised at just how easy it is to create something you're proud of, and how naturally the creativity flows. Your skill will improve the more you colour, and as you get used to using different tools and techniques.

Inside these pages you will find a stunning array of gorgeous flowers, including beautiful roses, stunning lilies, pretty peonies and fantastic floral designs – all waiting for some colour. Choose which element of the image you most want to stand out, what colours the petals and stems are, what the weather's like – there are no limits.

If the simple act of concentrating on colouring has a meditative, therapeutic effect, then there are also myriad reasons why flexing our creative muscles can only be a good thing. There are countless psychological studies that show the benefits of creativity – from reducing stress to decreasing the likelihood of depression, and even improving confidence and a more optimistic outlook.

One thing that puts many people off making art a part of their life is the time involved. The very nature of colouring books means they're perfect for modern life. A watercolour artist might need days in the field with an easel, a sculptor might slave for weeks in the studio over a single creation... but a book like this can be carried around with you as you go about your day, picked up and set down as needed, opened or shut as the mood takes. Any and every spare moment is an opportunity, whether you have five minutes or five hours.

An activity that's creative, that's good for your mental well-being, that helps relieve stress, reconnects you with your inner artist and improves hand-eye coordination and concentration and that you can carry around with you and dip into wherever you go? *Inspired Colouring* is all these things – and with every new creation you work on, the benefits can only increase.

Finally, a word about materials and techniques. One of the best things about colouring is that you don't need to splash out on a whole range of specialized materials or expensive equipment, and different techniques can simply be picked up (or ignored) as you go. There are no rules, and whatever you do can never be definitively declared 'wrong'.

Of course, having said that, it can be exciting to have an excuse to splash out on some new goodies – so if you do fancy a trip to your local stationery store or art shop, you could do worse than invest in the following:

Pencils – of varying grades – HB is the standard, but for finer, harder lines or crosshatching consider an H or even 2H, and for thicker, smudgier shadings a B, 2B or 3B.

Coloured pencils – a quality pack of just about every colour you could want will cost very little.

A pencil sharpener and rubber – for keeping things tidy.

Crayons/felt-tip pens/marker pens/highlighters/poster paints/whatever else you like – why not? If you think it might work, give it a go…

As for techniques, again there are no rules. Some people like to colour in blocks in the traditional way, others to use pencils to shade or cross-hatch (that is, to make a kind of grid of varying width and/or thickness to imply depth or shade). Still others might make patterns of their own design, or use felt tip in the outer corners of each section with pencils inside… the point is, do whatever works for you.

These are your designs and there is no right or wrong way of making them beautiful. The process of colouring in is at least as important as the result.

So relax, clear your mind, set free your artistic flair and enjoy the unique therapeutic effect of *Inspired Colouring*. And most of all: have fun!

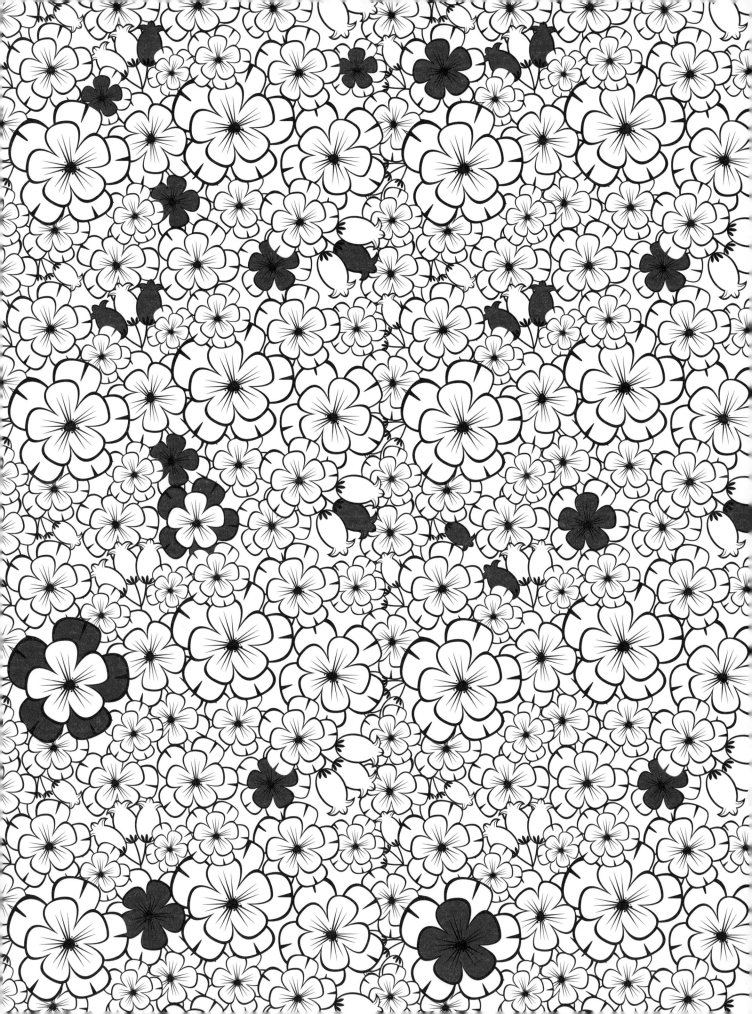

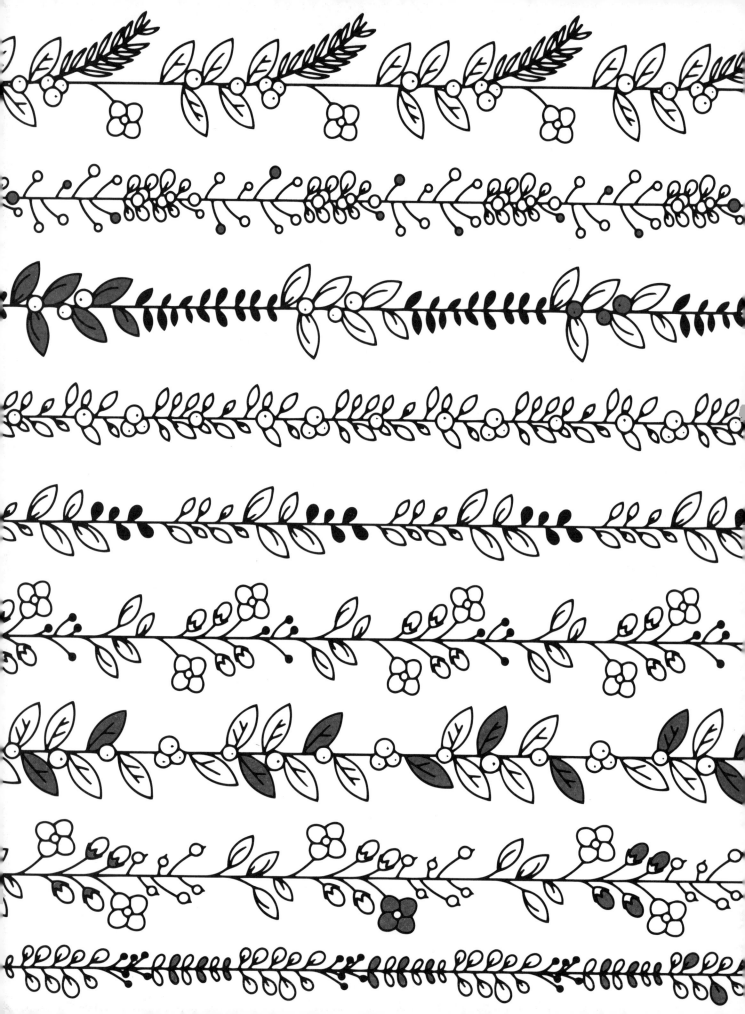